Coastlines of the Archipelago

Coastlines of the Archipelago

by

Colin Morton

BuschekBooks

Copyright © 2000 Colin Morton
All rights, including moral rights, reserved

Canadian Cataloguing in Publication Data

Morton, Colin, 1948-
    Coastlines of the archipelago

Poems.
ISBN 1-894543-00-9

    I. Title.

PS8576.O746C62 2000   C811'.54   C00-900156-5
PR9199.3.M656C62 2000

The aerial photograph (A 15044-35) that forms the cover image © 1999 Her Majesty the Queen in Right of Canada. Reproduced from the collection of the National Air Photo Library with permission of Natural Resources Canada.

BuschekBooks
P.O. Box 74053
35 Beechwood Avenue
Ottawa, ON K1M 2H9

The Canada Council | Le Conseil des Arts
for the Arts | du Canada

BuschekBooks acknowledges the support of the Canada Council for the Arts for its publishing program.

Acknowledgments

Many of these poems have appeared in the following periodicals, anthologies and websites: *The Malahat Review, Descant, Arc, The Fiddlehead, Stanzas, The New Federation, Ascent, The Florida Review, Chili Verde Review, Mankato Poetry Review, New Zoo Poetry Review, The Golden Section; Licking the Honey Off a Thorn, Whiplash Anthology 2, Witnessing the Earth, Tender is the Net, Minnesota Poetry Calendar 1997; Atmospherics, Recursive Angel, Realpoetik, Salt River Review, Blue Moon Quarterly.*

The jazz-inspired suite "Mood Indigo" was privately printed as a limited edition chapbook by Grove Avenue Press. Several of the poems appeared in the chapbook *Coastlines*, from above/ground press. "Settlers" and "Five to Midnight" appeared in In *Transit* (Thistledown Press); "Anniversary" and "The Weekend the Children are with their Father" appeared in *This Won't Last Forever* (Longspoon Press).

"Five to Midnight" and "Growing into the Culture" are dedicated to Jeffrey Morton.

For Mary Lee

Contents

At a Nameless Bend in the River 11
Overflow 12
The Gap 14
Tree Planting 15
Out by the Airport 18
Settlers 22
Serenade-Nocturne-Aubade 24
West Coast Revisited 26
Letter to an Old Friend 27
Promises in the Dark 28
Five to Midnight 29
Autumnal 30
Anniversary 31

Mood Indigo 32

The Weekend the Children are with their Father 44
Preparations for a Journey 45
Re:Crossing 46
Fireworks 51
Where Were You When? 53
The Passenger 54
Three Small Rooms 56
Lost Letters 57
Signs of Change 58
Growing into the Culture 59
To the Burgess Shale 62
The Return 67
The Coastlines of the Archipelago 70

At a Nameless Bend in the River

We don't understand the first thing
about most of what goes on around us.
The operating system
without which the disk drive won't boot.
The inner workings
of the sewage treatment plant downstream.

Currents that lead fish to this reedy spot
where we cast our lines from shore.
How to cleanse the putrid
streams of Eastern Europe.
How a dollar is still worth a dollar
after all that's gone down. Even this:

why at sunset white-tailed deer
come down to the river and graze
unconcerned at our presence
where all the parched afternoon
they hid in shadow.
The heaviness of flesh and bone
we dream of more often than hold, and hold
too tight sometimes, not quite believing. You.

The simple rise and setting of the sun
confound our pretensions. The way we still
dial a touch-tone phone, confide our secrets
more readily to pollsters than lovers.
How we can speak in any voice
other than our own. The constitution.
How the fish we counted on slip our hooks
and glide away into darkness.

The red sky is omenless, our string bag
empty. White-tailed deer
lie panting in a field of clover
under skeletal hydro towers.
On the far shore throbbing windpipes
unnumbered as leaves on the trees
sing the only tune they know
to the waning light.

Overflow

Ice heaves beneath my feet—a crack!—
and I edge flat-footed shoreward
aware of the fragile membrane between
my bloodstream and the deadly
current below: the barrier breached
by a rock some boy has thrown
or the beaver I watched last fall
come to breathe the upper air awhile,
straddling the gap the way a poem
breaches the gulf between silence
and speech, the quick hop-step
between dream and memory.

Once I forced my own fissures:
one rainy afternoon broke through
the stone wall of the old pig barn
with my cousin, loosened small stones
from chalky mortar and threw them
hard as we could against the wall
till larger stones fell, then picked up those
and threw again, exulting in the effort
till cracks of light shone in,
a wet gust hit our faces and
amazed at what we had done
we gulped the fresh air,
rubbed dust from our eyes
and climbed the rubble into daylight.

My ghost breath rises over the dike
that parts the river from the flats
where swollen currents used to
overflow their banks each spring,
invade basements, rot the roots of trees,
bring rats into backyards until
the planning department raised this wall
of "clean fill only"
that polluted the city's cleanest beach
—long before I first walked here
making plans of my own,
the future barely hinted
in the ripening twilight
that pierced the lower clouds.

Now my way ahead is deep in snow,
the ice behind won't bear me
—no passage sure but the future
breaking through on its way to the past.

The Gap

In the holes between memories
In the blind spot missed in the rear-view mirror
Through cracks in the walls
Under doors that don't quite latch
Between hands that don't quite touch
Filling the distance that opens with every goodbye
The gap spreads, the vacuum we always abhorred
But where we've been heading all along.

I have glimpsed it on occasion, still do—
More often, perhaps, since the time
I gazed in and nearly lost it
Drawn down in the undertow—the current
Of so much separation can drown—
The parting, the forgetting, the trembling
And settling of the earth that leave holes
In and between us. And we never

Learn. Here I am again gazing, half
Mesmerized by the dark invitation
To step out of the loop and forget, to let
The spaces between words spread out
As far as the margins, as if nothing
Could say as much as silence.

Tree Planting

Foot on spade, turn up the earth,
then slip
the seedling home,
move on three steps and begin again.
Stooping, digging, planting trees
all weekend long

we Scouts spread out along
a rocky ridge of earth
that defeated settlers decades ago. Tall trees
would grow from our slips,
the grownups said, and returning again
years later we'd find it home

to deer, fox, birds... *Home
on the Range, It's a Long
and Winding Road,* we sang again
and again as we stooped to the earth
and tucked under the scrawny slips
of seedling poplar trees.

Only we never did go back. We left the trees
to the elements and drove home
bringing a handful of leftover slips
I planted along
the side of the garage in earth
hard as clay. Once again

I stooped and dug, again
tucked under trees
the size of my hand, watered the earth
to make their roots a home.
Then I forgot them. Long
dry weeks went by and the slips

turning brown and brittle, slipped
my mind. When I looked again
only one survived—a long
gangly sapling, less tree
than weed—but it claimed a home
on that stretch of packed earth.

Dry winds, then frost—the earth
did its worst. Time slipped
through my fingers. I left home,
moved back again;
my fender scraped the tree
one night I stayed in the bar too long.

And all that was long
ago too. I've circled the earth
a few times since then, seen trees
many centuries old, sung *Slip-
sliding Away* and really meant it. Today again
I board a plane and find myself at home

or rather in my old home
town—Mom sold the house not long
after I moved out again.
Sometimes, as if to unearth
old memories that might have slipped
away, I drive by the old place and look at my tree.

Someone else's now, the tree
stands higher than the house we called home,
twice as high. I'd like to slip
over the fence, climb onto its long
white branches and feel the earth
turning as I lie and look up again

into the sky's blue depths, till I regain
whatever I've lost since planting this tree
—the sound of the wind, the smell of earth
after rain. The old home
has changed little along
the way, although the garage slipped

off its foundation, was torn down. Now slips
of poplar again
spring up in the empty space along
the alley, and the little tree
I used to drive over makes the home
look smaller than before. Earth

darkens as I watch, only the tops of trees
still bright. I sit in the car looking home
and wonder where else I belong on this earth.

Out by the Airport

1. Remember the future?

The *Star Weekly* features—
effortless households of 2001
their model city skyways always clear
and the color of a pack of Players?

We believed it!

Though we looked down the bomb-sights
of *The Twentieth Century*
and lay on our backs in the schoolyard
watching faroff vapor trails
of B-52s heading north

we grew up expert in self-deception
able to leap contradictions
in a single bound.

We cycled home from school
in the mad adventure of air-raid drill
supposing two minutes would save us
and we'd rise from the wreckage of our homes
to a life fit for heroes.

Summer nights in the schoolyard
far from city lights
we stared up at Polaris Cassiopeia
the Pleiades and talked
of the ages their light took to reach us
how we'd reverse that distance some day
and what we would find beyond.

2. Mythology

How much we left behind
believing we sprang full-grown
from our own foreheads!

Weightless amid the northern summer
constellations we named
everything we saw, spun
yarns round our legendary feats of
last year when we were kids

great escapes from Ken the grocer
breathless, laughing so hard
candy spurted from reddened mouths

our treks up Spy Hill or
along Nose Creek in search of hideouts

the night we counted forty UFOs
out where the highway passes the airport
and nearly burnt our lean-to to the ground.

    3. *Topsoil*

Salt drying on our backs
we lay against the hill's warm flank
foxtail stalks between our teeth
eyes swimming with cumulus plesiosaurs
fingers crumbling flakes of old seabed:
skeletons of bivalves alive here once
under other skies.

        Clover   mint   alfalfa   sage
        cutbanks   salt-flats   alkali ponds
        withered   grass   and   crusty   marsh
        a face scratched out by ice and wind
        on a shell of crushed bone.

That *barren* prairie—
how much we found there
digging in the clay, exploring
coulees dugouts storm sewers
ruins of lost cities.

4. *Fireweed*

Fireweed singes the eskers
along the embankment
where the dayliner skims Nose Creek.

Horses who gave their names
to boulevard and drive
don't graze this itching hide
of a barbwire short grass prairie anymore.

No hoof prints but golden arches
cover North Hill now
and the westerlies whine through signposts
blow through the daydreams of ones too young to know.

5. *Split Rock*

Overhead light years
underfoot centuries
pressed thin by glaciers

tumbled granite
worn smooth on the backs of bison
old men we know chased as boys
the length of this valley

where stock cars race now
instant fossils tipped over
the cliff behind the track.

6. *Weightless*

Bodies in motion, abject and free
falling
      —earth in its orbit

cosmonauts in capsules
the moment before re-
entry.

       We too
in our brief descent from jump shot
horseback, the second's

suspension before we curl up
and cannonball into the deep end
          —we too have felt that
                    freedom's tug.

Settlers

My forebears were well acquainted
with these distances
grew close to the prairie,
knew the wind tide in its grasses,
the cry of wildfowl deserting the frozen ponds.

On the run from another land's quarrels
to the periphery of power
they arrived on this unpromising plain and
began the search for water and a name.

The land lay flat in ambush,
made no response
to the advances of the plough
until it grew fertile with their blood.

Time was their own here.
Time to grow old and die.
Time aplenty to die without growing old
to smother in grain dust as a child
or fall from heat exhaustion
into the machinery.

They held to the earth like a wife.

Today the road spins out beneath the wheels
at ninety fenceposts hiss by,
dry streambeds wind through the fields
on either side of the highway embankment
until it is swallowed in a tangle of city streets.

At home near the outskirts I
recall only their horizons rolling back under steel,
how when the land picked up and blew away
they were rescued by their creditors
and put to work for wages

how they built the road back themselves
to the country they fled

lined up at the ticket office
to enlist in its wars

as now we tune in by satellite
and the distances dissolve.

Serenade – Nocturne – Aubade

1.

Edging off the map
    we have to learn
        to read the signs.

At a bend in the path
    you turned to go
        and shadows obscured
what I thought I saw on your lips.

A second late
    words found me
        and ever since
I'm saying them over.

2.

With a thirst nothing quenches
    holding onto words
        heard in a dream
I walk all night in the wind.

Isn't it enough to say
    I knew you when?

3.

Overnight snow crescents
    alight on the apples.
Jays, finches, chickadees
    spill seed from the feeder.
        Waxwings tipple.

The cat and I at our window
    watch them tumble
        stalking answers
if that's what I'm doing

spreading this trail down the page
    asking myself
        if it would be better
if we had never met.

West Coast Revisited

A day of travel, a night of talk
and laughter, old friendships renewed.

Near dawn I tumble down
a forest trail to be alone
in this place I always loved
for its derelict abandon.

Shells washed ashore, small broken spines,
trunks scored and stripped by tide.

The grey horizon, dawn mist rising
from the trees. The conversation
I came all this way for, the voice
that says "you too, you too" all night and day.

We never said it, did we? Face to face
in a night of smiles, each of us
thinking "like me, like me" and gazing
across the room, afraid we would miss

the one look we've been looking for
since we left our mothers' homes.

Letter to an Old Friend

As I remember you never gave up
what you set your mind to, dreamed a woman
without pity and, waking, followed her.

When you stood at roadside with thumb out and
tried to stare down the world coming at you
I knew, if I hadn't guessed already

you had something to prove and you wouldn't
give up till you proved it. To yourself
or me? Is there any difference?

I sometimes wonder, digging among papers
left behind, clues to the missing
last days, the cold dark matter surrounding

a few shining moments—one
you clung to like a cherished hypothesis
you could never prove. All those mixed messages

misplaced days. Remember how she thought
you had changed that time you met in the street,
how you gazed after when she walked away?

Promises in the Dark

> *Something was missing* I wrote years later
> *what could I do   I went looking* (all this
> before I met you).
> *First prayed to it*
> *then pointed a lens where I thought it should be*
> *all along inventing answers   destinations*
> *until old enough (or almost)*
> *I stood thumb out at the edge of the highway*
> *begging entry to dangerous dreams.*

You too used to walk those dry shoulders
hungry for more.
We might have passed each other often on that road
our eyes always on the way ahead.
Instead we met and hitched together
on a trip that started as a weekend
and has taken us this far.

> You spotted me
> crossing the campus fuzzy-headed
> listening to the echoes of dreams
> and calling them poems
> wearing a black button on my sweater
> —*Anarchists Unite!*

We came together
in the student union hall
—a poem you read me in another tongue—
made promises in the dark we believed
we would never have time to keep.

Five to Midnight

At last the storm is passing, or pausing
to restore itself over the gulf, clouds heave
a redolent breath on the rooftops,
and behind the closed door your howls
have ended,
         sleep
washes anger and fear from your face.

I stand over your bed twenty years
from an understanding with you,
knowing we may not have those years
or if we do today
will be dream time then to both of us,
become other people, translated
into foreign lives.

You won't remember this day and I
might say nothing happened.
We made it through the hours at home
on the bus and on
the hate/love rollercoaster ride of being five.
I listened to the news at lunch, dreading
to be out of touch another hour.
We put together your jigsaw puzzles
to show you had all the pieces,
you did a lot for yourself, did without
even me in the end,
                  as you will have to
some day we can't yet imagine.

The sky is impatient, tugged and tossed
in a mist of last roses
                 and above the rain
satellites plough silent cameras through
what is left of the twentieth century

almost everywhere on earth it is tomorrow.

Autumnal

October's breath ferments in the lane
fallen apples tomatoes on the windowsills

& everything's new again even first things
even birdcry the whitecaps' swell and lap

our first winter together leaves
blowing our questions scattered at our feet

half-familiar faces slips of paper reminders
stuck between pages found years later

urgent voices in sleepless houses (remember?)
our faces as they once were bright in the darkness

we walked each other partway home partway back reluctant
to give up the dead weight of night

the sweet weariness in our limbs our words
too late our shadows new as ever.

Anniversary

Such a long and heady time I lived in then,
in if, in abstract worlds without you
throwing words into echo's canyon,
my head in the electric blue.

A whole decade I rode a high
charged wire, all ecstasy and nausea
darting from sub- to super- to an image
of maybe, glimpsed in starlight.

Like some charged particle I was nothing
or nowhere, something or somewhere
never both, never here when most alive
nor quite myself when I
gave up into your darkness
the glimmering half-life before sleep.

That's why I still can't believe it
when, famished, spent, I return
to this cluttered, unsure, almost senseless
now, that is all the sense that lasts,
to test my feet on solid ground and find
you are still here, still
patient as time with a jet-lagged traveller

proving on the senses what's real
can't be caught in the striving nor
seen in the whirling radiance of hot words,
but grows in darkness and mess, in odd
loose days that, being in them, seem not to fit
but, touching now, grow into seasons, ripen
in secret to an unsuspected grace that
one day awakens us here, together.

Mood Indigo

Cool and blue
    a cool blue ball in the sky

As if we never saw us before
    the way we stare

A cool blue eye half lidded
    that won't stare back
        wouldn't care

What time of day
    we came or went

Cool blue
    me or you
        it's all the same out there

§

A horn gets it started
    that long sweet
        shudder on the air

No wall can stop it
    walls just stand there
        waiting to fall

The bones grow weary
    bread crumbles
        mortar dries

But the smell of home cooking makes
    everyone hungry
        especially a long way from home

§

What if this once you missed the last train
    would you stay with me

The way you looked at me just now
    I think you would

Ah let's forget the whole damn thing
    let the hours go

And if you take a shine to me too
    I promise you

You'll never need to chase
    that train again

§

Skatt-min   scat wind blow
from your apple tree limb
high in the sky up above

Whisper low fragrant föhn wind
fill up my barrelhouse lungs and
let me blow along beneath the trees with you

    Can it be because we're in love
        the sky is so tuneful
    so high up above us
        so blue

§

The road never turned
    any beggar away

So it must be the place
    for you and me

There's nothing it can throw our way
    too hot for us to handle

Nowhere we can't go
    if we go side by side

As long as there's Sunday
    there'll be Saturday night

As long as there's a sunset
    we'll have somewhere to ride away

Nothing we're leaving is
    too big to carry

But I'm betting we'll need both hands
    for what's ahead

§

Maybe Monday
    maybe someday
I'll get over being homesick
    for the days when I was lonesome
        before I met you

Oh the world was smaller then it's true
    we weren't so used to feeling lost
still thought we could do some good
    looking under the hood
        of the Oldsmobile

I didn't miss you then you see
    my whole life lay ahead of me

§

My heart keeps running back to you
    the way it did the first time

Remember
    back in New Orleans

You arrived on the four-thirty train
    and who was there to meet you

In the cold predawn
    —just me

Remember the night
    the power went out

But we had all we needed
    each other

§

Just you   just me
    remember how it used to be

We'd wake up neighbors on our way home
    jamming with the roosters

You'd make coffee and I'd read you
    the funnies before the reviews

Just you   just me
    in our attic on the sunny side

I love the way we used to be
    before all that shit went down

§

You tell me we're all riding
    an escalator to the gallows

Don't you think I know
    how much you're hurting

But for all that I can do
    you might be howling at the moon

Calling out their names
    the ones you've lost

I see you drink your poison neat
    I'll have mine with a twist

§

Funny I don't feel much different now
day rises bright as ever before

But I won't be catching that train again
won't be paying you calls any more

I always thought we were part of His plan
but I guess you didn't see it that way

I wanted to show you where I grew up
and secretly hoped you would stay

But if it must be I can live this way
at least let me walk you to the door

§

Never thought our differences
    added up to much beside the rest

But have it your own way go on
    I never said I couldn't live without you

We won't see each other
    on the street anymore

Won't linger over coffee
    you won't touch my hand

When I light your smoke anymore
    but we'll meet again

Some day I'm sure
    we'll sit down for coffee together again

For an hour have nowhere
    we would rather be

We dreamt so long
    of this freedom day

Call it farewell then never adieu
    I prefer to think of it that way

§

As if anyone could find
       let alone define the life of night

Of dark of blue the true
       sound that could spell an end and again a beginning

As if you signed your name
       in every word you said

As if any name on a treaty signified
       any mark any seal any assignation
in the rainy square outside the railway station

Anywhere you say I'll meet you there

§

You didn't even wait to say goodbye
but you know I can be stubborn too

Though with everything that we've been through
you'd think we'd find a better way

Sometimes I just feel like dying
sometimes I think I've come to love
this hurt you left behind

Sometimes I say to hell with it
I'm going and I don't care where
just know I'm getting out of here

§

Through the café window a far
cedar avenue waves in the wind

Through coffee-steamed glass
across rain-slick blacktop
beyond the red taillights of late afternoon

Through the mist the cedars recall
the grainy war-time photo
that used to hang over our breakfast table

An instant startled in the aperture
moments before the storm

§

I haven't been home in so long now
      don't remember what I looked like then

Would anyone know me if I returned
      would they tell me where you're living

I might hang around catch a glimpse of you
        maybe running for the train

The way you used to when
      you'd spent the afternoon with me

Who knows you might even be humming
      one of our old tunes

§

I dreamt you with
        the Statue of Liberty's face
                half-buried in sand

Bent my ear as if
        I knew how to get the truth
                out of oracles

Learned about what
        you'd expect from a stone

Walked all the way home with a burn and
        a mouthful of sand

§

Fee fie
        free I
                come a come come
aren't it isn't I eh

A quizzical one
        am ear eye
                stand by
the blues have moved in to stay

§

And if you did come back
    if you walked in my door one fine day
when I've finally stopped waiting and made a new start
    would I take your hand

O I know I've been through this
    too many times before
stayed home too many nights in case you called

Still if you did come back
    and found me waiting

If you stretched out your hand to mine

§

So much about you
    I almost forgot

Even the twist you give your smile
    the child's laugh in your eye

So much the years have stolen
    even from our dreams

So many hot nights it will take
    to rub feeling back into hands and feet

To step out onto the streets where we live
    and make a new start

§

Together again arm in arm
    still swinging the way we used to
        can it be so long ago

Before the war when Paris was Paris
    and you and I never missed a beat
        or ever went to bed before dawn

So long ago we almost forgot
    how to kiss

So here's a big one
    for all those years

§

It's all right now
I'll be better in a little while

I guess I just wasn't ready
to see you walk through the door

I'm not about to make a scene you know
in fact I'll soon have to run

Drop me a line if you're passing through town
we'll meet somewhere and reminisce

No harm in calling anyhow
if only to say hello

§

So this is why
      victory needs wings

To keep rising farther out of reach
      beyond question

Secrets aloft on a high
      slow fadeout to mute

Now the walls with all
      their echoes are gone

Do you hear the children's voices
      and what can be that eerie sound

That far faint lonesome reverb
      still ringing in my ears

The Weekend the Children are with their Father

The dreams of modern lovers are set in shopping malls
where they walk as if at the seashore listening to the sweet muzak of
    the tide rolling in

and the young woman tries on shoes at competitive prices
    in a half dozen stores
but the heels are all too high or blockish the toes too square or
    round

and as the dream goes on she becomes rounder too
not only her breasts but also her hips and especially her eyes

they stroll hand in hand down the gourmet aisles in the
    supermart
but come away with only one bruised yellow apple or
    mango or pomegranate

wrapped in cellophane reduced to clear
which she will eat later in the seclusion of her bed

and both are vaguely dissatisfied as they wander out to the parking
    lot
having forgotten which car they came in not only where they left it

and the good neighbor collection box is just too appealing
the thought of all the less fortunates makes her eyes mist
    over like the sea at dawn

and the woman can't resist crawling inside
but the hatch doesn't open wide enough to let her man follow

and standing outside totally engulfed in fog now
he can hear nothing but the sound of the half-spoiled
    apple crunching softly between her teeth.

Preparations for a Journey

I won't be able to drive all the way.
I'll reach a point too deep in mud,
the road so narrow
overhanging branches scratch the windshield.

I'll have to carry on my back
whatever I bring with me,
lash together whatever will float
to ferry me.

I'll find some island or mountainside
overlooking all approaches

or a cave so well sheltered
I'll hear nothing but the rush of blood
from heart to head,
see no colours but as in memory.

At a bend in the river
where currents pause and circle
on their way to the sea

or a coastline scoured by tides
bearing remnants of lost continents

or in this cave of light
amid the dark streets
silent at last toward dawn

I'll scratch at the page
till I feel them fight free
—the words to begin again.

Re: Crossing

5/20/96

Drive south into spring
where May snow shelters on the forest floor,
cross the border and drive out from under
into hazy interlake Ontario

roosterruled farmyards composed like Flemish masters
      door/dogdish/bone/halfton/compact/trike
      sugarbush/pigtrough/railfence/ditches blooming

snapshots of lives that never stand still
long enough to know.

5/24/96

In the bulk food store:
a bin of pencil stubs,
a stack of ecoposters
printed one side only.

I wrote a letter home a letter away a letter home and so on
until I ran out of paper and
all the letters I had to write
were away away away.

5/26/96

I drive the wide arched
bridge over the Seaway and down
the valley in the road's hypnosis.

Beneath me flows the wealth of Chicago Detroit
and all the prairie states—*la fleuve*
opens like a French kiss to the Atlantic
trading lanes.

Granada/Panama/the Gulf/Somalia
even Bosnia at last—wherever
an American has interests
the marines will mobilize in days.
How long do you suppose to secure a seaway
two hours from the Statue of Liberty?

I ask this of a radio caller
once outraged at the sight of a tank.

5/28/96

Citizen A veers across three lanes of traffic
to thrust a poster in the face of Citizen B
ignoring B's child in her wobbly stroller
       and politicians talk of amiable divorce
            —*Calice!*

A people so angry a cyclist brakes
to argue with the ones he nearly hit
speeding under the bridge
... over the edge no matter.

In early evening hot air balloons drift overhead
little moons reflecting sunset over the green plain
over a city of rivers/spires/streetpeople

brainy people with no idea
people of two minds who go years without writing a letter
people hardy in their foolhardiness
people who say *but but but but*
beautiful people skin deep
with their past imperfect
passive-aggressive possessives
sociable people with significant others
who dream of leaving it all behind

If I could say *my people*

5/30/96

I walk your sidewalks again
no wider than last year
and rather than smile as we pass you look away
make me a negative integer,
a cataract, a blank on your screen.

I jaywalk, forget to wear a hat
leave my umbrella on the bus
stand in front of a deputy assistant in an elevator
and feel the fear like rain.

Averting eyes we make of each other
the negative image of a country
too busy to look

        up/over/around/through into
        out   about

6/3/96

I have tried sometimes as tourists say
pénétrer la vie des gens
outside my own door,
have tried to know these reluctant people
so much part of me.

Headlines land like grenades on doorsteps each morning
but the joggers aren't home, they're out with the newsboy,
sleek thighs delivering them
round the leafy lagoon and home to showers
while my coffee cools on a windowledge
overflowing with pencil stubs.

They pass my window running/walking
on cycle/skateboard always somewhere
backpacking grade schoolers
inline skating/online surfing high school juniors
retirees fending brooms
young mothers with childseats on bicycle fenders.

Who wouldn't have a soft spot for them?
deputy assistants in blue and red
power suits already sweat-stained
on the way to the bus stop with *Globe* under arm,
though more cynical the more they understand
of anything they read.

I know their clumsy minds lost transitive grins,
have heard my own hollow echo
theirs in a goodbye hug.

These folk so unclaimed they refuse to be called folk,
free people
with their silence and immense disappointment
arrogant people hugging resentments like stuffed toys
people of ice and irony
who know the cost of everything but silence
close-lipped people lonely as indefinite articles
who have never been asked to forgive before.

6/4/96

The cost plus tax plus tax plus
the gross cost

6/6/96

Some welcome home if
that's what you call it
—a head turned away
and this blank page.

6/24/96

Joke or prophecy?
Rain falls so hard car alarms cry out
all over Parliament Hill.

"Having read this book
tie a stone to it and throw it in the river
lest what is written here shall come to pass."

After rain the forests between us incense the air
with birth and death, copulating blooms
and hot air balloons drift by and on the river
hatchlings kick boldly into the current.

We meet on shore,
each with a bag of crusts
to spread on the water.

Fireworks

Though not for love of country
(unless summer is a country)
one year we joined the crowds
and hopped a free bus to Parliament Hill,
stood hip to thigh with blue-jeaned students
—smoking drinking filling the aisles
with hoots at the *hunks* and *chicks* on the sidewalks,
ignoring the strangers beside them.

Patriots for a day
they tried to rouse a chorus of *O Canada*
but couldn't agree on the words
or language,
though all roared together at last
the *Brady Bunch* theme.

Stepping down on Queen
we joined the sidewalk throngs
—our city alive at last—
walking toward the hill, the flame,
the big screen music video images
of our Olympian heroes.

Other years too we have stood arm in arm
in the oohing ahhing crowd
till the last flare, bang and sizzle.

No more or less for love of country now
we stay around home,
walk only a few moments at last
to stand on a ridge over the canal
where long after the flash
has faded and smoke begun to disperse
the report arrives—low thud
of far-off thunder—no thrill
for our neighbors' sleepy children.

None for me either—
before the last flash I'm ready
to walk on through this mild night,
stroll the hospitable streets toward home
where a champagne cork is
fireworks enough for us tonight.

Where Were You When?

When I was just fourteen and
played on the team first string
I was horny as hornets and JFK
was my ideal (I admit it now)

but hey—"He was my brother"
who fell that autumn during playoffs
put graveyards not goalposts on the front page

and though I wandered out hotter than ever after
I half-knew I'd get no satisfaction on those icy streets
a half-step short of the sad end of love.

Now in DC decades later I visit
not Arlington but the wall, sunken tombstone
of space age innocence, brothers and sisters
who lay down for the echo of a memory of a lie

for the hero who is always too human to rule
for the peace these pilgrims carry away in their tears
for what balm they may deliver.

The Passenger

1.
Light catches in the tails of snow foxes
that chase each other down the road.
I walk against the wind believing
help may be under the yardlight
of the farm I saw in passing
just before I misjudged the curve.

2.
I arrive and find a party going on.
I warm my back by the fire and return
the indifferent smiles of guests
well advanced in drink, hors d'oeuvres and gossip.
Hot cider, they offer. *Good
for what ails you, bottoms up.*

3.
Marzipan titbits—little human ears,
noses, hands and feet. *How long
since you've eaten?* How far
have I travelled dreaming I'd find you
standing in a room like this
in front of a full-length mirror?

4.
Here, sign the guest book.
I'm documenting the occasion. Already
my folder of clippings is bulging.
I have snaps of the desktop
where this is happening.
I call it *poésie verité*.

5.
Down a dim corridor
like others in this mansion
I follow a big red setter
I met begging scraps from the table.
I've thrown him a finger, a bitter
big toe. Ask *him* where we're going.

6.
Have you ever hiked in the desert?
It's nothing like here
where the forest is so like a house
even now in uncurtained November.
Our true shape, I believe, is a sphere
or pandimensional ellipse.

7.
Back at the party, the shovelmouths
haven't even slowed down. Early arrivers
carry their stomachs in shopping carts.
Singing waiters dispense their folk
philosophy: *Shrimp or salmon,*
your choice is absolutely free.

8.
She's alive, she's real, you won't
believe your eyes, they sing.
But I know they couldn't mean you
who found me once by the road
trying to dance feeling
back into my frozen feet.

9.
I woke on the floor, staring up.
My bruises cried out for sleep.
I remembered failures, resentments
gaffes, missed chances, empty triumphs.
Not him, I heard behind me. *He's not the one*
I want to find in the mirror.

10.
Breaking surface I gasp and
feel solid ground underfoot.
I lunge ashore and lie watching flames
of wreckage reflected on water.
Where is she? Where? I cry. But searchers
find no sign of a passenger.

Three Small Rooms

1. *Kyrielle*

How we found this room I do not know.
I dreamt of it last night, I'm sure
Someone will come any minute now
And tell us what we're waiting for.

Out the window all I see is snow.
It's getting far too cold in here.
Go tell them we have far to go
And ask what we are waiting for.

2. *Roundel*

In this empty room we gather
The reports of all the blind men
Without asking how or whether
In this empty room
These tales of snake or tree or fan
Can be reconciled together.

We mix guesses, lies and half-lies, then
From the ludicrous palaver
Try to sort out truth from lie again
And start the conjuring over
In this empty room.

3. *Triolet*

In a room without windows
We peer at photos taken in the dark,
Eerie blurred shadows
In a room without windows
Portraits of ... who knows?
Posed smiling somewhere in a park.
In a room without windows
We peer at photos taken in the dark.

Lost Letters

Our letters are all suspended
between destinations

Bs and Cs far from any coast

Es denuded of accents
settling to the bottom of the sack

redirected to places mentioned only in books
with geographies and histories unheard of

where songs have no words and no words sing

where things have no names or names
that flit across borders as if all one

countries of stone countries of water
where harvests lie buried in snow
like the words of a book never opened

countries where a signature is a kiss.

Signs of Change

We've gone this way before, should know its turns
but suddenly we're lost. At the edge
of a marsh where blackbirds nest in the reeds
we watch for signs—a broken twig, a whiff
of smoke, a face turning from a window.

Out on the long distance line a lightning-
split pole has touched the ground. Our voices
like empty bottles thrown from car windows
rattle in the wires.

There's no end of talk, no end of indirection.
Cataclysms inside distant galaxies
don't move us. They're borders away, orders

beyond the visible band. Graffiti
scrawled at the swampy north end of the bridge

declare: endless love, *No Future Now*.

Growing into the Culture

You're part of it now

must always have been, at least
I saw no beginning. Since

you unlearned your first
reflex to grip with your toes
you have always been kicking

deep into our world.
You were at it already
sitting on your mother's knee,
taking it all in.

Scared of the wolf at the door,
you rode your dreams through Mirkwood,
cried out in the night
trusting someone would be there
to let you know you were safe.

You woke to the news
reports of overnight deaths
on the radio, the song
of birds outside your
window proclaiming the sky
and all the treetops their own.

If you saw them you
would want to count—*Amazing
Numbers*—you wore that book out
reading it over
each night instead of sleeping.
When I came to tuck you in
you always stumped me

with *The Riddles of the Sphinx*
then sang yourself to sleep with
Bach's G-minor fugue.
Later, bored in grade five, you
wrote equations on your arms,
collected coins, stones,
pieces of metal you found
walking home from school. You turned

your bedroom into
a lost-and-found museum,
papered your walls with pages
from an old Escher
calendar, and as in them
fish turn into birds and stairs
descend as the eye
climbs with them, you kept changing,
growing into the culture.

Then you discovered
The Computations of God.
We telecommunicate
by them now. Our words
speed through fibre optics, but
like your eye level, you have
travelled far beyond
our once-common ground, become
a metamagical star.
On your nth return

from planet Transylvania,
you're certain reality
is what you can get
away with; you wear the proof
etched into your skin with ink.
Late at night we raid
the fridge together, argue
for its own sake, the changing
value of X. You

took your own name and called it
down a rabbit hole into
cyberspace, then you
made your own system, without
any threat you'd be enslaved
by another one.
They're out there accessing now—
all your mind children—transformed

into some wild, wired
hallucination I'll have
to stop calling the future.
You've been part of it
all your life, and it doesn't
scare you. Our eyes meet over
the tops of our books

and you act annoyed that I
keep on looking, just as if
you don't know all this
will soon be over and past.
It's your nineteenth birthday, Jeff,
and I'm writing this

because next time we may be
too rushed—one of us or both
stopping off between
flights just long enough to say
hello—our lives veering off

in opposite ways—
these loose-ended days no more
than a fading memory
then—the mirror where once

we saw one another smile
become a computer screen
where we write what in

real time we can hardly speak.
And look: though we've come so far,

we're still beginning.

To the Burgess Shale

Foothills

i)

Before the sun appears the loons
call across the water, and robins
belligerent in the dew, bicker
among the drowsy sparrows.
Horses sleep standing, turned to the fragrant westerlies
shift foot to foot in the midst of a dream.
All night's cicada continuo
syncopates with the long-beaked
oil pumps' click and hiss

bobbing and rising all night.
They plunge, draw back—
the bulky shadows' minimalist dance
sends black dot-dashes down the pipe
from a time before mountains
before anything we know but this
dance of light and shadow across the moon—

dawn's glint off distant icecaps,
strobe against passing windshields
on the parkway interchange,
greasy gleam on the crown block
sliding into earth, lustreless
diamond biting Cambrian shoals,
the whole slick spectrum ashimmer on the blacktop,
the blinking liquid crystal saying *You'll be late.*

ii)

Earth, water, blood
the scent of smoke.
Dawn hoar frost points
scrawny fingers at the sky.
Mountains dream moon faces
in shadows of cloud on water
moon faces in the cinders
ochre and ashes
sand in the corners of eyes.

iii)

> *High above the Yoho River...snowbound from the middle of October until the first week in July ... the collection of fossils is prohibited.*

Night's a journey by sea with skeleton crew.
A new day breech-delivers.

So this morning I pack up the trunk,
strap skis to the roof of the car and go west
leaving only the echo of an empty room,
my initials in the sidewalk
on the street where I grew up.

iv)

Leave at daybreak if you hope to arrive before dark and you should.
Leave at dawn on a full tank of gas,
you never know when you'll see neon or
or have any use for your plastic again.
You're going where snow is centuries deep and fierce
wild flowers fight their way skyward
after a light just out of reach.
Walk slowly, don't strain.
This air isn't used to you either
or your voracious lungs.
Find a rock and sit, look up at the blue
ice caps then down at the small
goings-on in the valley you thought so urgent.
Take a long look before going on.

Precipice

v)

From a distance it sounds like a busy highway
or some great engine set to work in the forest.

Approaching the falls, you taste on your lips
the spray you didn't know till now
if you imagined.

At its foot the earth shakes, blood pounds and
—luminous exhaust—all the colours of the day
cling to your lashes.

vi)

Yesterdays pile up faster than tomorrow.

> *yohoia   habelia   anomalocaris*
> *wiwaxia   opabinia*

Sinew me Lord
    if it be among your powers

Give me abs of steel and cover me with skin
    then breathe in life if you can.

Pour over me healing baptismal blood
    then set me free
to walk this valley of bones alone
    in search of a friend or a home.

> *amiskwia   marella   canadaspis*
> *naraoia   hallucigenia*

Life signs written on stone
in the language of the dead.

vii)

We stand on a peak amid whitecaps
seabed at our feet
all shifting sands,
and watch our shadows creep
across the strata
till they merge with night.

For a week beyond radio
high in the mountains
we go without
knowing the number of dead,
the hourly alarm
no more than a breath of butterfly wing.

Whatever we may lose
in the climb to this edge,
we bring home more than we find here
—more than we could ever carry.

viii)

A naked ape doesn't look so bad
standing next to a naked man.
He reaches out and gets it
—no excuses—and when he slips
he falls. Evolution:
this comedy of grab and run.

The all at once is all.
You don't need a rear-view mirror
to see what's in front of you.
Every creature knows it, every slug in the mud.
It would take a rare fool not to—
an ingenious fool

to put on a mask and scare himself silly.
Fool enough to call himself a fool
and laugh.

The Return

I hadn't shaved yet and already I couldn't remember
where I was born. I went back to see
but there was no *where* there:
all the houses torn down
the road signs changed.
Pigeons lived in the rafters of the station
and I was in such a rush
to trip over my feet and land in clover
I wrote a bad poem every day.

Each day I stopped too soon and went out looking
and sometimes I found what I went for
sometimes not and I didn't always care.
Sometimes to go was the thing itself.
Sometimes the street was mine and vice versa:
the trees, the river, the windows
and chimneys of the houses along the streets and river,
and sometimes the light on the windows was enough,
sometimes the gleam on the waves and
the hair of passing women, their flashing legs.
Sometimes nothing was enough;
no hole deep enough.
I shut my doors and went about blindfold
but always even blind I was looking.

I still had all my hair
and my beard was red but I didn't know where I was born.
I went to Expo wanting to belong,
but there was Man enough, world enough already.
I lay on the flank of Île-Ste-Hélène
and felt warm and alone all over,
and the Seaway carried me away
holding hands with a shy queer inside his coat pocket
while fireworks lit up the river at La Ronde.

The Transcanada was an unreeling tape
with my feet slap-slapping
and glaciers and oceans and gold
fields of wheat, and I took my bad poetry everywhere,
smuggled it through the mails,
pried uncancelled stamps off envelopes
and sent them out again to seek their fortunes
as I sent my self out again and again
turned everything over just to see.

I swam in the Aegean on New Year's scheming
how to breach the Iron Curtain and get away East
—ate guest workers' bread, drank comrades' *aqua vit*
all the way across the Balkans with two Swiss francs in my pocket.
Next night lay under a bridge and talked of dying and
never felt so transcontinental.

Returning you remember by way of Niagara
we crossed another continent, we thought
there would always be another and we
would always be
just on the verge of disappointment
as the train was always on the edge
of a forest it could never be part of
as we thought disappointment would always be
part of us not vice versa.

Three days and three nights that far that far away.
We felt like death but that was nothing
to what we felt for each other
under the flimsy railroad blanket
sitting up all night in coach
while lakes and fields and mountains rolled away beneath us
on the point of spilling over
the edge of exhaustion all night
in the hack clack clattering of the track
growing farther and farther from the sea—

Moose Jaw, Swift Current, Medicine Hat.
Paint it gold and red and infrared
as smoke of forest fires bleeds the sunset
and we roll steadily, steadily farther away—

Grand Banks, Mount Royal, Agawa, Batoche.
The rivers wind in no hurry now,
the cattle pad the lean prairie,
a lone halfton crosses a dark ridge, its taillights
flickering like fireflies in the distance.
We have thrown ourselves out and out and
now we're nearly home again—

the dry lands, badlands, irrigation locks
packing plant, trailer park, rocky horizon.
And sometimes the engine's cry at crossings brings a tear
and I wish—
I wish I was starting over
and could throw myself out again
to see who drifts back and when
I try to slide out to the bar car
just before arrival
you wake up beside me and hold on
and I know it's happened already, we've done it
come back to where we were
and started over.

The Coastlines of the Archipelago

measure infinity

the next moment's act
is fractal

in a day a century's
monuments topple
a year's events
depart so far from what
we thought we knew
how it all came about

by infinite trajectories
within a little space

must long be mystery

but what a strange attractor
that must be

(   )

the wave is on the out
to hazardous vastnesses

seacoast
river's outline
the branching of trees
"a glittering in the veins"

galaxies in the scaling zone of sizes

turbulence

word frequencies